Mao Tse-tung was a modest man. He was a man of the people, a man of peasant simplicity. He was also "by far the greatest man in the world today—probably the greatest of this century", as the historian A. L. Rowse wrote in 1975, a year before Mao's death.

Mao's greatness lay in his simplicity. The Chinese people, poor and oppressed, saw in him the father-figure they desperately needed. He was a romantic revolutionary. He won admiration in the adventures of the Long March. He was a fine poet—and he had a powerful vision of communism in China. He knew that with the faith of the Chinese people in him he could achieve anything. He won that faith, and led them to become one of the world's most respected and feared nations. Yet he was not without enemies or critics.

Hugh Purcell's fascinating biography of Mao shows the character of the man and the qualities of the leader, set against the background of the most extraordinary era in China's long history. This book is an essential aid to the study of modern China.

More than fifty illustrations, list of principal characters, table of dates, reading list and index.

Mao at his cave headquarters in
Yenan, 1944.

WAYLAND HISTORY MAKERS

Mao Tse-tung

Hugh Purcell

Wayland Publishers Limited / Hove, England

More Wayland History Makers

The Last Czar W. H. C. Smith   *Joseph Stalin* David Hayes and F. H. Gregory
Hitler Matthew Holden   *Captain Scott* David Sweetman
Goering F. H. Gregory   *Jomo Kenyatta* Julian Friedmann
Lenin Lionel Kochan   *The Borgias* David Sweetman
Karl Marx Caroline Seaward   *Martin Luther King* Patricia Baker
The Wright Brothers Russell Ash   *Bismarck* Richard Kisch
Cecil Rhodes Neil Bates   *Rommel* F. H. Gregory
Picasso David Sweetman   *Cromwell* Amanda Purves
Al Capone Mary Letts   *Franco* Richard Kisch

ISBN 85340 406 2

Copyright © 1977 by Hugh Purcell
First published in the UK in 1977
by Wayland (Publishers) Ltd, 49 Lansdowne Place,
Hove, East Sussex BN3 1HS
Second impression 1979

Contents

List of Illustrations

1. Mao the Romantic Revolutionary

In October 1966 Mao Tse-tung inspected a mass meeting of the Red Guards (China's youth movement). The following report of the meeting appeared in the *Peking Review:* "At ten minutes past one the majestic strains of 'The East is Red' [a popular Chinese anthem] were struck up, and the happiest moment which people had been looking forward to day and night had arrived.

"Chairman Mao, our most, most respected and beloved leader . . . together with other leading comrades of the party centre, rode in nine open cars. . . . Loud bursts of joy roared from the square. Countless hands waved dazzling copies of *Quotations from Chairman Mao* and countless pairs of eyes turned towards the direction of the reddest red sun. Shouts and cheers of 'Long live Chairman Mao!' thundered forth. . . .

"Many students quickly opened their copies of *Quotations from Chairman Mao* and wrote the same words on the flyleaf: 'At 1.10 p.m. on 18th October, the most, most happy and the most, most unforgettable moment in my life, I saw Chairman Mao, the never-setting red sun.'"

To us this report might sound rather comic. It might sound rather sickening, too, but it is an illustration of the hero-worship which surrounded Chairman Mao. Yet Mao was a modest man. In speech, dress and manner he was a man of the people, a man of peasant simplicity. So why did he encourage this hero worship?

> **"People of the world, be courageous, dare to fight, defy difficulties and advance wave upon wave. Then the whole world will belong to the people. Monsters of all kinds shall be destroyed."**
> *From* The Thoughts of Chairman Mao.

Opposite Mao on a visit to his old school at Shao Shan, 1959.

Above Mao repeating his Yangtze swim in 1966 at the age of 73.

Perhaps the ancient Chinese philosopher Confucius can tell us the answer. He was once asked by a ruler what three things were needed to rule well. He answered that first, the people should have enough food to eat; second, they should have enough military power to protect themselves; third, they should have faith in their ruler. When he was asked what should be left out if only two of these were possible he answered that the military power should be omitted. When asked further what should be left out if only one of these was possible he answered, "Let them lose their food and keep their faith in you."

Mao knew that he needed the faith of the people, just as the people, whose ancestors for centuries had worshipped their emperor, needed him as a father-figure. He also believed that with the faith of the people behind

him, anything could be achieved. He once wrote: "China's 600 million people have two remarkable peculiarities; they are first of all poor, and secondly blank. This may seem like a bad thing, but it is really a good thing. Poor people want change, want to do things, want revolution. A clean sheet of paper has no blotches, and so the newest and most beautiful words can be written on it."

Mao probably understood his people with more shrewdness and ruled them with more cunning than any other modern leader. And who can deny that Mao did use the faith of the "poor and blank" people, so that by the time of his death in 1976 China had become a mighty nation?

Another of Mao's famous sayings is "Dare to think and dare to do". He put this into action in 1957 by

Above Red Guards from all over China gathering in Peking to see their Chairman in 1966.

swimming across the eleven km (seven miles) wide river Yangtze. He was then sixty-four years old. Afterwards he wrote a poem about it:

I care not that the wind blows and the waves beat;
It is better than idly strolling in a courtyard;
Today I am free!

There is a political meaning behind this verse. Mao is saying that because he is in the midst of a struggle he feels alive and free. In fact Mao struggled all his life against one enemy or another, as he tried to make life better for himself and the Chinese people. When he was a child he struggled to escape his peasant background by leaving home and educating himself. When he was a young man he struggled to protect the new Chinese Communist Party against the ruling regime, the Kuomintang. Then, in middle age, he led the Chinese communists in a fourteen-year war; first against the Japanese invaders and then in a civil war against the Kuomintang. In 1949 his victories took the communists to power over the whole of mainland China.

After that, despite growing old and losing his health, Mao pitched the Chinese people into a further quarter-century of struggle. This took two forms. First, he waged a peacetime war against mankind's oldest enemies—poverty, disease and ignorance. Second, he led a crusade to establish communism—that ideal state where everyone works according to his ability, receives according to his needs and, in return for giving up his possessions and labour for the common good, ends up by ruling himself.

Ideal states are rarely achieved, and China is still a long way from a state of pure communism. Nevertheless, right up until his death Mao sustained a vision and struggled to make it a reality. For this reason the Chinese people gave him the title of "romantic revolutionary"—one who "dares to think and dares to do".

Opposite The Empress Dowager of China and her attendants.

2. Mao the Peasants' Friend

Mao Tse-tung was born on 26th December, 1893, in a little village called Shao Shan, in the central Chinese province of Hunan. He was the eldest of three brothers and one sister, children of a rich peasant called Mao Jen-sheng. Mao's father owned one and a half hectares (three and a half acres) of land. This was enough to enable him to hire a few labourers and make money by selling his surplus rice and vegetables. This is all the children ate, although their diet was spiced with red peppers. Mao liked chewing them so much that his friends nicknamed him "The Red Hot Pepper".

Mao was always quarrelling with his bullying father, who followed the saying of Confucius that children should obey their fathers and subjects should obey their rulers. Mao argued back by choosing other classical quotations which said that elders should be kind and affectionate! For this cheekiness he was often beaten and more than once he ran away from home.

When Mao was seven his father sent him to school. He was taken away from school at thirteen and set to work managing the farm accounts. Now he was considered an adult, and the next year he was married. But for Mao, being an adult was no substitute for being educated. He left his wife and persuaded his father to let him go back to school—this time to the primary school at Hsiang Hsiang, 24 km (fifteen miles) away.

Here Mao was teased because of his poverty. He was

Above The house in Shao Shan where Mao lived as a boy, from 1893.

Opposite A wealthy family at home, about 1870.

15

called "the dirty little peasant from Shao Shan". The school library, however, more than made up for this. He was often the first to arrive and the last to leave. Mao once said that a library to him was as appetizing as a vegetable garden to an ox!

At his next school Mao made one firm friend, Siao-yu. Together they spent their holidays wandering about the Hunanese hills. They walked stripped to the waist, eating little food, sleeping rough and bathing in the mountain streams. From an early age Mao delighted in physical toughness. By the time he was eighteen he had developed a love of learning and a sense of duty to the poor peasants. He wished to become a teacher and improve their lives.

At the time of Mao's childhood over ninety per cent of China's people lived in the countryside. Their lives consisted of back-breaking work and endless suffering. There were four main reasons for this. First, natural disasters like floods, droughts and crop failure were almost yearly events in one part of China or another. In 1887–88, for example, a famine in northern China killed ten million people.

Second, the population of China was growing enormously. In 1866 it was 400 million; by 1972 it had grown to 800 million (nearly one quarter of mankind). This meant that the land per head was decreasing, so that each year there was less for each person to eat.

Third, the peasants were very badly treated by the landlords who owned the land on which they worked. Over half of China's cultivated land was owned by about ten per cent of the population. In 1927 Mao toured Hunan province and reported that the poor peasants, numbering sixty-five per cent of the population, owned between ten and fifteen per cent of the land. Seventy per cent was owned by landlords, rich peasants and money-lenders.

The landlords had a stranglehold on the peasants.

The landless workers were dependent on them for employment and the tenant farmers were dependent on them for their land. The landlords were also the tax collectors, money-lenders and store-owners. It was easier to make money from the peasants than it was to become good farmers. To show their contempt for manual work they wore gowns with long sleeves covering their hands and grew very long finger-nails.

Finally, the peasants were crushed by taxation. Frequently the peasant could not pay his taxes without borrowing money. Once in debt to the landlord or money-lender he found it almost impossible to repay him. For example, one peasant borrowed 60 kg (130 lb) of beans from his landlord. Three years later he had paid back over 900 kg (2,000 lb) of wheat and 450 kg (1,000 lb) of corn; but the landlord was so greedy that he still wanted more.

It seems that the tradition and splendour of Chinese civilization was matched by a total disregard for human life. A western traveller, Edgar Snow, who witnessed a famine near Mongolia in 1929, wrote: "In those hours of nightmare I saw thousands of men, women and children starving to death before my eyes. . . . But these were not the most shocking things of all. The shocking thing was that in many of those towns there were still rich men, rice hoarders, wheat hoarders, money-lenders and landlords, with armed guards to defend them. . . . In the cities where officials danced or played with sing-song girls there was grain and food. . . . .

"Yet the great majority of those people who died did so without an act of protest. 'Why don't they revolt?' I asked myself. 'Why don't they sweep into the great cities, and plunder the wealth of the rascals who buy their daughters and wives, the men who continue to gorge themselves on elaborate thirty-six course banquets while honest men starve?'

"I was profoundly puzzled by their passivity. For a

"**What is the greatest question in the world? The greatest question is of getting food to eat. What is the greatest force? The greatest force is that of the union of the popular masses.**" *From* The Political Thought of Mao Tse-tung *by Stuart Schram.*

"**It is not that we [the Chinese] have no strength; the source of our impotence lies in our lack of practice. For thousands of years the Chinese people of several hundred millions have all led a life of slaves. Only one person—the 'emperor'—was not a slave, or rather one could say that even he was the slave of 'heaven'.**" *From* The Political Thought of Mao Tse-tung *by Stuart Schram.*

17

Above A busy street scene, about 1870, showing a scribe, a fortune teller, a soup seller, a physician and a barber following their trades in the open air.

while I thought nothing would make a Chinese fight. I was mistaken. The Chinese peasant is not passive; he is not a coward. He will fight when he is given a method, an organization, leadership, a workable programme,

hope—and arms." The Chinese peasants were ripe for
rebellion, and were only waiting for a leader. Although
they did not know it, they were waiting for Mao Tse-
tung.

3. Mao the Young Politician

In 1911 Mao left Hsiang Hsiang to go to the middle school at Changsha, the capital of Hunan province. It was now, for the first time, that he became involved in political affairs.

In China 1911 was a year of great events. The most dramatic of them was the revolution which, the next year, led to the abdication of the last Chinese Emperor, the six-year-old Henry Pu-yi. Until 1911 the emperors of China, called the "sons of heaven", ruled as absolute dictators. There was no council or parliament to keep a check on them. They delegated authority to officials known as "mandarins", who were themselves dictators in their own provinces. The mandarins made the laws, raised the taxes, ran the police and controlled the law courts. So with the landlords at the bottom and the emperor at the top, China was ruled by a series of dictators, most of them corrupt.

The revolution in 1911 was known as the "double ten", because it was begun on 10th October—the tenth day of the tenth month. It was organized by the Revolutionary League (later named the Kuomintang) led by Sun Yat-sen and a group of army generals. Both Sun Yat-sen and the generals wanted to get rid of the emperors because they were dictators who used their power badly. But they were not prepared to tackle China's basic problem. This was to give more land and more rights to the peasants who made up ninety per

Above Sun Yat-sen, China's new leader, in 1912.

Opposite Hankow in 1911. Two thousands troops and a gunboat were called in to protect the European quarter after rioting broke out.

21

Above Henry Pu-yi, China's last emperor. He abdicated in 1912, aged six. After the Japanese conquered Manchuria, they made him its emperor from 1934–45. He died in Peking in 1967.

cent of China's population.

When Pu-yi was overthrown in 1912 China was divided. North China was reduced to a state of anarchy by the "war-lords". These were army generals with their own private armies who, having united to overthrow one corrupt dictatorship, merely replaced it with scores of others. Each war-lord seized control of his own area and squabbled with his rivals. South China was ruled more sensibly by Dr Sun Yat-sen and the Kuomintang.

Sun Yat-sen was a Christian revolutionary who had been educated in the west. He gradually came to realize that the only way to unite China was to make a complete break with the old order. He summed up his ideas in the "Three People's Principles". These were: democracy (which meant overthrowing the emperors and introducing a democratic political system); socialism (which meant taking the land from the landlords and giving it to the peasants); and nationalism (which meant freeing China from all foreign control). These Three Principles appealed strongly to the young Mao. As an early gesture against the emperors and their traditional ideas, Mao and a friend went around clipping off their fellow students' pigtails (known as *queues*). Mao hated these *queues* because they were a symbol of submission to the emperor.

What roused Mao's anger as much as the exploitation of the peasants was the exploitation of China by foreigners. Because of Chinese weakness and western greed, by the beginning of this century almost all Chinese foreign trade and ports were controlled by the Americans, the Japanese, the French, the Russians, the British or the Germans. China's wealth was also in the hands of foreigners, who controlled the railways, commerce, banking and the silk industry. Not content with managing China's wealth, the foreign powers stole its territories as well. Great Britain had taken possession

打鬼燒書圖

狗尾妖書如糞臭
謗聖賢毀仙佛
九州四海切同仇

豬精邪叫自洋倫
欺天地藏祖宗
萬醉十刀難抵罪

Left An anti-western cartoon shows Chinese scholars holding their noses while they burn foreign books and peasants attacking westerners with farm implements.

of Hong Kong, France had taken Indo-China, Japan had taken Korea and Russia had expanded into central Asia.

These foreigners rubbed in their power by treating the Chinese as servants. In Shanghai, Mao discovered, the Chinese were even treated like animals. A notice at the entrance to the main park said: "No admittance to Chinese or dogs." Mao hated this arrogance. He said sarcastically: "If one of our foreign masters farts, it's a lovely perfume."

So from early manhood Mao supported two of the Three Principles—socialism and nationalism. He became a dedicated follower of Sun Yat-sen. He told Edgar Snow years later that at this time he "wasted no words on love or romance and considered the times too critical and the need for knowledge too urgent to discuss women or personal matters". He was soon to disagree with Sun Yat-sen, however, over the third Principle—democracy. For Mao was about to become a communist.

> **"We often say 'The Chinese government is the counting-house of our foreign masters'."** *From* The Political Thought of Mao Tse-tung *by Stuart Schram.*

> **"The force at the core leading our cause forward is the Chinese Communist Party. The theoretical basis guiding our thinking is Marxism–Leninism."** *From* The Thoughts of Chairman Mao.

4. Mao the Communist Rebel

In 1918 Mao Tse-tung went to Peking. He was struck with the beauty of the city and his poetic nature found an outlet in this description: "In the parks and the old palace grounds I saw the early northern spring; I saw the white plum blossoms flower while the ice still held solid over the North Sea."

Mao started work in Peking as a lowly library assistant at Peking National University. He was so poor that he shared a room with seven others. "I had to warn people on each side when I wanted to turn over," he remembered later.

At the University Mao met Professor Yang Ch'ang-chi, who introduced him to western philosophy, and the librarian Li Ta-chao, who introduced him to communism. Mao also met and married Yang Ch'ang-chi's daughter, which shows that he was not such a dedicated student as he liked to think.

Mao and his fellow students were inspired by the Russian Revolution and eagerly read the works of Karl Marx (1818–83, a German who founded modern international communism). Mao said of the communist books he read: "They built up in me a faith in Marxism from which, once I had accepted it as the correct interpretation of history, I did not waver."

Over the next two years Mao came to realize that peaceful protests, whether on the streets or in illegal newspapers, were of no use in the struggle to free the

"Our principle is that the Party commands the gun, and the gun must never be allowed to command the Party." *From* The Thoughts of Chairman Mao.

Opposite Mao in Shanghai in 1924, at the age of 31.

25

Above The Forbidden City, Peking, as Mao saw it as a student in 1920.

"If there is to be a revolution, there must be a revolutionary party.... Without a party built on the Marxist–Leninist revolutionary style, it is impossible to defeat imperialism and its running dogs." *From* The Thoughts of Chairman Mao.

peasants from oppression and remove foreign domination from China. He and other students increasingly looked towards communism for the answer.

In July 1921 the First Congress of the Chinese Communist Party was held in Shanghai. There were only thirteen delegates, of whom Mao was one. What was to be the policy of the CCP? At first it was decided to form a "united front" with the Kuomintang in order to overthrow the war-lords in north China and to establish a national government. This policy suited Mao, whose main wish was to see a strong united China. He was more concerned with nationalism than with communism, as he would be throughout his life. It also suited Sun Yat-sen. He said: "We no longer look to the west. Our faces are turned towards Russia."

Sun Yat-sen died in 1925 and with his death the "united front" collapsed. The fault lay mainly with the

new Kuomintang leader, Chiang Kai-shek. He was more interested in power than in the Three Principles. As a result he decided to drop the second principle of socialism (thereby winning the support of the wealthy classes) and drive out the communists.

In April 1927 Chiang put his treacherous policy into action by ordering his troops to massacre the unsuspecting communists in Shanghai. Similar massacres were carried out in many other towns, until the CCP was broken. In 1928 he entered Peking and declared himself the new ruler of China with the title of Generalissimo. Many of the remaining communists left the CCP after Chiang declared that membership would be punished by death. One of the communists who was executed at this time was Yang K'ai-hui, Mao's second wife.

For Mao, however, this disaster turned out to be a blessing in disguise. Had the "united front" not col-

Above Cavalry troops under the command of General Chiang Kai-shek riding through Canton, 1925.

"**Thousands upon thousands of martyrs have heroically laid down their lives for the people; let us hold their banner high and march ahead along the path crimson with their blood.**"
From The Thoughts of Chairman Mao.

> **"This army has an indomitable spirit and is determined to vanquish all enemies and never to yield. No matter what the difficulties and hardships, so long as a single man remains, he will fight on."**
> *From* The Thoughts of Chairman Mao.

lapsed it is possible that communism in China might have developed as it did in the Soviet Union. It might have taken root in the towns and taken hold of the country after a civil war. This, in fact, remained the aim of Mao's comrades. They started to prepare the town workers for the overthrow of the Kuomintang regime. Mao, however, had different ideas. He disagreed with the party line and decided to go his own way. By so doing he laid the foundations of Chinese communism.

Mao was convinced that any communist revolution should start in the countryside. One day, he predicted, "several hundred million peasants will rise like a tornado-force so extraordinarily swift and violent that no power, however great, will be able to suppress it."

The question was, when? Mao soon came to realize that any mass uprising at that time would be overwhelmed by the powerful Kuomintang army. So he decided to build up his forces slowly and surely and avoid a head-on civil war. Knowing from his boyhood wanderings that the mountains of Hunan and Kiangsi were excellent ground for guerilla warfare, he planned to withdraw to the hills and set up base areas, or "soviets". In these soviets, these states within a state, Mao would win the peasants' support by improving their lives and then train them into "Red Armies". (Red is not only the traditional colour of revolution, but also to the Chinese it signifies joy.) These armies would capture and destroy the Kuomintang forces.

Mao defended his strategy by using an earthy—and effective—simile. The "base area", he said, bore the same relation to an army as did the buttocks to a person. Without them, one could never rest, but would have to run until exhausted!

In 1929 Mao formed his first soviet at Kiangsi, on the border of Hunan. It survived deep inside Kuomintang territory for five years.

> **"The sole purpose of this army is to stand firmly with the Chinese people and to serve them wholeheartedly."**
> *From* The Thoughts of Chairman Mao.

28

Opposite Karl Marx, whose works inspired Mao when he was a student.

5. Mao the Bandit Chief

By 1934 there were six separate soviets north and south of the river Yangtze, covering a population of nine million people. The largest soviet was Kiangsi and Mao was its chairman. He had also been re-elected to the ruling committee of the CCP by his comrades, who now realized the weakness of communism in the cities compared to the strength of Mao's soviets in the countryside.

It was now that Mao Tse-tung began to emerge as a pioneer of modern guerilla warfare. Indeed his methods were later studied not only by revolutionaries in such countries as Cuba and Vietnam but also by the forces sent to defeat them. To soldiers everywhere he became a great source of inspiration and instruction, just as he was to politicians. The famous British soldier Field-Marshal Montgomery said once: "Mao is the man to go into the jungle with!"

Mao's theories of guerilla warefare were specially worked out for the Red Army. The Army lived by the rule book and, like so many rules in Communist China, military rules were converted into songs and slogans so that everyone would remember them. First there were the eight rules of discipline:

1. Replace all doors when you leave a house and return the straw matting [wooden doors were easily removed and were used as beds].
2. Be courteous to people and help them when you can.

"Apart from the role played by the Party, the reason the Red Army can sustain itself without being exhausted ... is the thoroughness of its democratic practice. The officers do not beat the soldiers; officers and soldiers have the same food and clothing and receive equal treatment." *From* The Political Thought of Mao Tse-tung *by Stuart Schram.*

Opposite Mao in Red Army uniform, 1936.

3. Return all borrowed articles and replace all damaged goods.
4. Be honest in all transactions with the peasants.
5. Be sanitary and dig latrines at a safe distance from homes and fill them up with earth before leaving.
6. Don't damage crops.
7. Don't molest women.
8. Never ill-treat prisoners of war.

Below Guerilla training in Northern China. Until they captured enemy weapons, they had to fight with spears and swords.

Mao knew that good discipline led to popular support, and the very survival of guerilla forces depended
on the support of the local population.

Then there were the four rules of tactics:

1. When the enemy advances we retreat.
2. When he escapes we harass.
3. When he retreats we pursue.
4. When he is tired we attack.

Below Kiangsi Province, where
Mao set up the first Chinese
soviet in 1929.

As Mao knew only too well, the Red Army was vastly inferior to the Kuomintang forces in manpower and materials. His tactics were designed to convert weakness into strength, relying on speed and mobility. Outright warfare was to be avoided; in a pitched battle the Red Army would be overwhelmed. But a short attack when the enemy was unprepared was a different matter, particularly when the Red Army was stronger. As Mao said: "The most important single tactic, therefore, was the Red Army's ability to concentrate its main forces in the attack, and swiftly divide and separate them afterwards."

Finally there were the three duties:

1. To struggle to the death against the enemy.
2. To arm the masses.
3. To raise money to support the struggle.

Mao used words like "struggle" and "arm" in a wider sense than the purely military. He considered that the soldiers' duty was to fight on the political front as well as on the battlefield. It was the Red Army's job, in fact, to mobilize every member of society for the revolution. This is still an important part of its duties today.

The first task in mobilizing the Chinese peasantry was to win their support. This the Red Army set out to do by a method which we might call "brain-washing", but which the Chinese call "thought reform". "Thought reform" means submitting the people to a constant diet of lectures, discussions and slogan-chanting in order to train them into "correct thinking". No doubt this "thought reform" was effective, but the Red Army really won the support of the poor peasants of Hunan and Kiangsi by driving out the landlords, sharing out their property and allowing the peasants in the soviets to have a say in the way they were governed. As a Kiangsi peasant explained to Edgar Snow: "He told me that his parents were poor farmers, with only four mou

> "The Kuomintang is the most faithful running dog of Japanese imperialism and the Kuomintang militarists are the greatest traitors in all Chinese history." *From* The Political Thought of Mao Tsetung *by Stuart Schram.*

> "We the Chinese nation have the spirit to fight the enemy to the last drop of our blood, the determination to recover our lost territory by our own efforts, and the ability to stand on our own feet in the family of nations." *From* The Thoughts of Chairman Mao.

34

of land [less than half a hectare or one acre], which wasn't enough to feed him and his two sisters. When the Reds came to his village, he said, all the peasants welcomed them, brought them hot tea and made sweets for them. The Red dramatists gave plays [obviously as a technique of thought reform]. It was a happy time. Only the landlords ran. When the land was redistributed his parents received their share. So they were not sorry but very glad, when he joined the 'poor people's army'."

> **"In times of difficulty we must not lose sight of our achievements, must see the bright future and must pluck up courage."** *From* The Thoughts of Chairman Mao.

Left The provinces of China.

> **"There are no straight roads in the world; we must be prepared to follow a road that twists and turns."** *From* The Thoughts of Chairman Mao.

35

6. The Long March—I

In 1930 Chiang Kai-shek, determined to crush the communists, launched four major campaigns against the soviets. The Red Army used Mao's guerilla tactics successfully, and beat back all four. Many thousands of Kuomintang forces deserted to join the communists.

Chiang's defeats, however, merely increased his determination. In 1933 he prepared nearly half a million troops for one final attack. This time he used different tactics. Instead of rushing into well-laid traps his troops surrounded the communists with blockhouses linked with barbed wire. Slowly the circles were tightened; hundreds of thousands of Kiangsi peasants were transported away or executed and the land was laid waste. Those left within the communist areas starved to death, for few supplies could be taken through the iron circle. Perhaps one million peasants died during this campaign.

The Red Army now changed its own tactics, making a desperate situation disastrous. Against the advice of Mao and his fellow guerilla leader Chu Teh, the other communist leaders ordered the Red Army to fight several outright battles to defend the cities. The Red Army was heavily defeated and after a year's fighting was reduced from 180,000 to 100,000 men. Mao said later: "We panicked and fought stupidly."

With the other soviets about to collapse and the iron circle around Kiangsi squeezing his people to death,

> **"Proud and alert, they carry five foot guns,**
> **The first rays of the morning sun illuminate the drill-field,**
> **The daughters of China are filled with high resolve,**
> **To red garments they prefer the uniform."** The Women's Militia, *from* The Political Thought of Mao Tse-tung *by Stuart Schram.*

Opposite Chiang Kai-shek.

Above At the end of the Long March. Soldiers from the Red Army arriving in northern Shensi.

"An army without culture is a dull-witted army, and a dull-witted army cannot defeat the enemy." *From* The Thoughts of Chairman Mao.

Mao made an agonizing decision. After six years of fighting he decided to abandon his hard-won soviet and make a do-or-die attempt to break out of the ring of destruction. And so in October 1934 Mao Tse-tung and Chu Teh, with ninety thousand men and thirty-five women of the Red Army, started on one of the truly epic journeys in the history of the human race. So began the Long March.

At the time Mao's only thought was survival. Afterwards he told the western journalist Robert Payne: "If you mean did we have any exact plans, the answer is that we had none." Mao at first only intended to march a few hundred miles north-west to another friendly soviet but he was driven further and further westwards by Chiang's army. It was only when the Red Army crossed the river Yangtze and its tributary the Tatu that they felt safe—for the time being.

Then Mao decided to put the survival of Chinese communism beyond doubt by marching his men a

further huge distance to the remote province of Shensi in the north. He knew that in this desolate, mountainous area a small soviet was already in existence far away from Chiang's army. As Shensi was near the Japanese border, Mao's plan to march there was of even greater importance to the marchers. Although the Red Army were depressed by retreating from one enemy their morale was lifted by the thought that they were marching towards another. The Long March thus changed from a desperate retreat into an advance towards victory.

Mao began the march by carrying all his possessions on his back. These were: a sun helmet; two uniforms; two blankets; a rice bowl and a torn umbrella, together with a pack containing his maps and papers. For the next four years the office of Chairman Mao was to be a cave, a wooden hut or just a canvas shelter.

The Red Army broke out of the iron circle after suffering huge losses from air attacks and pitched

> "Reading is learning, but applying is also learning and the more important kind of learning at that.... It is often not a matter of first learning and then doing but of doing and then learning, for doing is itself learning." *From* The Thoughts of Chairman Mao.

39

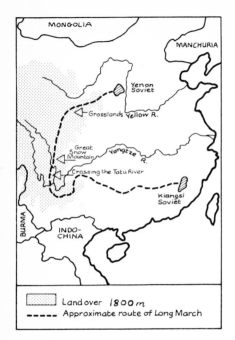

Above The route of the Long March. Much of the 10,000-kilometre journey was in mountainous country.

40

battles. One historian has estimated that these losses cost nearly fifty thousand men—half the Red Army. For the next few months the communists marched westwards, with the sole intention of shaking off the Kuomintang.

Then they turned north to cross the Yangtze and its tributaries. It was now that they had one of the most exciting adventures of the Long March—the crossing of the Tatu River. With Chiang's forces close behind, the communists had to cross the river or be killed. The nearest bridge was over 160 km (one hundred miles) along the Tatu gorge. They marched along narrow cliff-top trails with a sheer drop into the river below, fighting off Kuomintang troops all the way.

When they arrived at the footbridge they found that the planks had been removed. The gorge, which was three hundred metres (yards) wide, was spanned by thirteen chains swaying above the rushing torrent far below. The other side of the dismantled bridge was guarded by Kuomintang troops with machine-guns. Here a few planks had been left in place. Twenty-two Red Army volunteers, armed with hand grenades and knives, set out to swing themselves across the chains and capture the other side. Agnes Smedley (a western journalist who met the survivors not long afterwards) takes up the story: "The army watched breathlessly as the men swung along the bridge chains. Ma Tu-chiu was the first to be shot into the wild torrent below. Then another man and another. The others pushed along, but just before they reached the flooring at the north bridgehead they saw enemy soldiers dumping cans of kerosene on the planks and setting them on fire. Watching the sheet of flame spread, some men hesitated, but the platoon political leader at last sprang down on the flooring before the flames reached his feet, calling to the others to follow. They came and crouched on the planks, releasing their hand grenades and unbuckling their swords.

"They ran through the flames and threw their hand grenades into the midst of the enemy. More and more men followed, the flames lapping at their clothing. Behind them sounded the roar of their comrades, and, beneath the roar, the heavy thud, thud, thud, of the last tree trunks falling into place (these were used as substitute planks). The bridge became a mass of running men with rifles ready, tramping out the flames as they ran. The enemy retreated to their second line defences. . . ."

At the Tatu River the Kuomintang thought they had the Red Army trapped "like fish in a bottle"; now the fish had escaped and were not going to be caught again. One stick of dynamite at the bridge moorings and the story of Chinese communism would have been very different.

The Long March established Mao's leadership of the Chinese Communist Party, for it was his spirit and vision that had sustained the Red Army. His military tactics were at last proved right too. At the conference of Tsunyi, held during the march, the CCP passed Fourteen Resolutions. These included one which said that the old slogan "not an inch of soviet territory to be lost" was "a total mistake". It was replaced by Mao's view that "for victory, we must not refuse to give up some parts of the Soviet territory and even to withdraw our main forces." Mao was elected Chairman of the CCP at this conference. He held the post until his death forty-one years later.

The Long March also spread the fame of the communists throughout China. By coming into contact with the Red Army, hundreds of thousands of Chinese who had not heard of the communists at all, or who regarded them as just another gang of bandits, came to admire their ideals and bravery.

7. The Long March—II

Although the Kuomintang had now been left behind, they still plagued the communists with air attacks. Hostile tribes were a menace, too. The main enemy now, however, was the Chinese countryside itself.

Ahead lay a 5,000 m (16,000 ft) pass over the great snowy mountains of western Szechuan, and many mountain ranges lay after that. Lin Piao (one of the other leaders of the march) had a weak heart and only just made it; Hsu Meng-chiu, whom Mao had appointed to tell the story of the March, had both feet amputated because of frostbite; Mao, ill with malaria, was carried on a stretcher. A survivor describes the crossing of the main pass: "Heavy fogs swirled about us, there was a high wind, and halfway up it began to rain. As we climbed higher and higher we were caught in a terrible hail-storm and the air became so thin that we could hardly breathe at all. Speech was completely impossible and the cold so dreadful that our breath froze and our hands and lips turned blue. Men and animals staggered and fell into chasms and disappeared forever. Those who sat down to rest or to relieve themselves froze to death on the spot. Exhausted political workers encouraged men by sign and touch to continue moving, indicating that the pass was just ahead.

"By nightfall we had crossed, at an altitude of 5,000 m (16,000 feet), and that night we bivouacked [camped] in a valley where there was no sign of human life."

"An ancient Chinese writer said: 'Though death befalls all men alike, it may be heavier than Mount Tai or lighter than a feather.' To die for the people is heavier than Mount Tai, but to die for the exploiters and oppressors [the Kuomintang] is lighter than a feather." *From* The Thoughts of Chairman Mao.

Opposite Chiachin Mountain, which was crossed by the Red Army on the Long March.

> "To win country-wide victory is only the first step in a long march.... The Chinese revolution is great, but the road after the revolution will be longer, the work greater and more arduous." *From* The Thoughts of Chairman Mao.

Then they came to the Great Grasslands, a vast swamp stretching for hundreds of miles over the Chinese–Tibetan borderland. Tall, wild grass covered a swamp of black mud and water several metres deep. The weather was wet and freezing cold. The only food was wild vegetables and herbs and men were reduced to drinking urine. No human habitation was seen for ten days, and the Red Army had to bribe guides to show them the narrow paths across the mud. At night they slept standing up, leaning against each other.

They had less food to eat now than at any other time on the Long March. Since there was no firewood anything they found had to be eaten raw. One survivor remembered that when they emerged from the Grasslands they were so hungry that "we began eating rats. We cleaned every village of rats. They tasted awful but we ate them."

The survivors of the Red Army finally made contact with the local Red forces in Shensi on 25th October, 1935. Only five thousand of the original marchers were left—only one man in twenty had come through. The facts of the Long March were extraordinary. The First Front Army covered 10,000 km (6,000 miles) in 368 days—an average of nearly 27 km (17 miles) per day. The main force averaged one skirmish per day and fought major pitched battles for 15 whole days. The marchers crossed 18 mountain ranges, 5 of them permanently snow-capped, 24 rivers and 12 provinces (each larger than most European countries). They broke through the enveloping armies of 10 provincial war-lords. They evaded or defeated more than 300,000 Kuomintang troops. They captured 62 cities. They penetrated areas through which no Chinese army had gone for many years. The isolation of these areas gave Mao his oddest experience of the march: "We came to places where so few people had been before that if you waded into the river, the fish would leap into your hands."

Mao's toughness had saved him and luck had protected him from injury in battle. He said afterwards that the women had showed more courage than the men. He was thinking, particularly, of his third wife, a teacher of eighteen named Ho Tzu-chen. Early on she was injured in an air attack, when eighteen pieces of shrapnel lodged in her body. Then she was forced to leave their three children along the way; she must have realized, rightly, that she would never see them again.

Near the end of the Long March Mao wrote a poem in which he referred to the Kuomintang as a "grey dragon". The grey dragon of the Kuomintang was still breathing fire, but after the achievements of the Long March, its slaying was in sight.

"**The world is progressing, the future is bright and no-one can change this general trend of history.**" *From* The Thoughts of Chairman Mao.

Below Mao and Chu Teh (right) at Yenan in 1938. Chu Teh commanded the First Front Army during the Long March. Later he became Vice-Chairman of Communist China. He died in 1976.

8. Who Was Mao Tse-tung?

Mao chose as his headquarters in the province of Shensi the town of Yenan. Here a river runs through a deep gorge. In the cliff face formed by the gorge Mao built a cave city for some twenty thousand people, with living quarters, hospitals and a military university. This Red Army university, said Edgar Snow, was "probably the world's only seat of higher learning whose classrooms were caves, with chairs and desks of stone and brick, whose blackboards were walls of limestone and clay, and whose buildings were completely bomb-proof". In this underground city, deep in the heart of friendly Shensi, Mao was able to nurse his weary followers back to health, safe from the Kuomintang.

During these years in Yenan Mao Tse-tung emerged as a public figure, both in China and abroad. Until now he had been regarded as a bandit chief or a revolutionary hero. Now, thanks to Edgar Snow, Robert Payne, Agnes Smedley and other western journalists who made the long trek through Kuomintang lines to Yenan, a fuller picture emerged. Indeed, the Chinese themselves learned about Mao from Snow's book *Red Star Over China*. This was translated into Chinese and included Mao's autobiography which he dictated to his western guest.

When Edgar Snow came face to face with Mao in 1936 he found: "A gaunt ... figure, above average height for a Chinese, somewhat stooped, with a head

> **"Free choice must be the basic principle of every marriage."** *From* The Political Thought of Mao Tse-tung *by Stuart Schram.*

Opposite Mao at Yenan, 1942.

of thick black hair grown very long, and with large, searching eyes, a high-bridged nose and prominent cheek bones."

A few years later Robert Payne watched him at a play put on by the Red Army in Yenan: "There was the heavy, leonine head, with blue-black hair, very thick, muscular shoulders, a long, smooth forehead, the spectacles glinting and his hands braced against his knees.

Below Students at Lu Hsun Art Academy, part of the Kangdah Cave University, practising songs of resistance.

One can tell more about a man from the way he enjoys drama than from observing him elsewhere. What was strange was that he was wholly feminine, reflected all the gestures of the actors, pursed his lips when they sang, made his mouth into a square when they were roaring with anger, and gently waved his arms when the firecrackers exploded.''

Mao set himself apart from people, which perhaps made it easier for him to make ruthless decisions. The Russian leader Nikita Khrushchev (1894–1971) compared Mao to Joseph Stalin (the ruthless dictator of Russia between 1924–53): "Like Stalin, Mao never recognized his comrades as his equals. ... When, in his opinion, a piece of furniture—or a comrade—became worn out, he would just throw it away and replace it."

Agnes Smedley said that she found Mao faintly repellent. Perhaps this was because he prided himself on his peasant origins and went out of his way to appear down-to-earth. When it was smart to have short hair, Mao grew his long. When it was considered affected to smoke, Mao smoked all the time, making an unpleasant sucking noise as he did so. When not smoking he chewed red peppers—the habit he had in childhood. He slouched along like a peasant in the field, wearing baggy trousers with his socks round his ankles. Once, when he was talking to Edgar Snow on a hot day, he took his trousers off altogether in order to feel more comfortable.

Mao took delight in adding to his peasant image by using earthy language. Yet it would be quite wrong to regard him as an insensitive and illiterate man. He was a fine poet and a keen reader who said that he counted a day wasted if he had not fought a battle or read sixty pages. He was also something of a philosopher.

Mao had a romantic side to his nature. As a young man he spoke out strongly against the traditional Chinese custom of forced marriages and hailed "the great wave of the freedom to love". At Yenan he prac-

"His face was rather large ... his nose was flattish and of a typical Chinese shape. His ears were well proportioned; his mouth, quite small .... He walked rather slowly, with his legs somewhat separated, in a way that reminded me of a duck waddling. His movements in sitting or standing were very slow. Also, he spoke slowly and he was by no means a gifted speaker." *A description of Mao in 1911 by his school friend Hsiao-yu.*

tised what he preached by divorcing the faithful Ho Tzu-chen, who had borne him five children, and marrying a film star known as Lan-ping, or "Blue Apple". Much later, as Chiang Ch'ing, she was to play a prominent part in Chinese politics.

Like many other contemporary political leaders such as Winston Churchill and Joseph Stalin, Mao preferred to work at night and rest during the day. Sitting in his simple cave with only one window and door he would write and read. He was an obsessive worker, as this account bears out. It refers to Mao writing his essay *On Protracted War*, in 1938: "For the first two days he did not sleep at all, working continuously by the light of a pair of candles and sometimes overlooking his meals. . . . By the fifth day he was perceptibly thinner and his eyes shot with blood, yet he still ignored food and went on writing. On the seventh day he was so engrossed that he failed to notice that the fire was burning a hole in his right shoe. Suddenly he jumped to his feet in pain, burst into laughter and asked, 'How did that happen?' He then drank a little wine and . . . plodded on until the essay was finished on the ninth day."

Mao was a peasant leader, an expert guerilla, a self-taught communist and a fine poet. But behind these roles lay a complex personality which Edgar Snow, who knew Mao over a period of thirty years, described as a mixture of peasant cunning and intellectual depth. It was this mixture that appealed to the Chinese people. As a peasant he was one of them. As a tough soldier he was always in the front line. As a teacher he was able to inspire. As a politician he was able to lead. These qualities enabled him to pull the Chinese people through a quarter-century of war and push them through a further quarter-century of revolution.

Opposite Yenan children helping to build an extension to their school.

9. Driving out the Japanese

In 1932 the Japanese, eager to expand their empire, conquered Chinese Manchuria. This northern province had belonged to China for three hundred years and produced vital supplies of coal, iron and grain. By 1938 the Japanese occupied all the major population centres of China like Peking, Shanghai and Canton and controlled most major industries.

True to his nationalist beliefs Mao decided to put the defeat of Japan before the defeat of the Kuomintang. Indeed, he even proposed an alliance with the "entirely hateful" Chiang Kai-shek and his supporters under the banner "Chinese do not fight Chinese!"

Chiang rejected this offer and sent an army to exterminate the Yenan soviet. Then events took a number of extraordinary turns. Chiang's troops refused to attack Yenan—they wanted to attack the Japanese instead. When Chiang visited the capital of Shensi in order to deal with them, they captured the Generalissimo and delivered him to Mao! But Mao, instead of executing his treacherous enemy, made a deal with him. He promised to end his campaign to overthrow the Kuomintang; he promised to stop the confiscation of landlords' land; he even promised to put his Red Army under the direction of Chiang's government. In return Chiang had to agree to an armistice and a joint attack on the Japanese. So Mao and Chiang united in a common struggle for "the three great objectives of national

> **"All reactionaries [capitalist countries like the USA] are paper tigers. In appearance the reactionaries are terrifying, but ... from a long term point of view, it is not the reactionaries but the people who are really powerful."** *From* The Thoughts of Chairman Mao.

Opposite Chinese soldiers marching along the Great Wall during the war against Japan.

Above Mao talking to two of the youngest soldiers in the Red Army at Yenan in 1939.

independence, democracy and freedom, and the people's livelihood and happiness''.

Making these concessions to Chiang showed that Mao put the well-being of China before everything else. Unlike many other dictators, including Chiang himself, he did not want to grasp power for himself.

Although Chiang Kai-shek regarded the last two ''great objectives'' with cynicism, it must be said that for a time he tried bravely to achieve the first. He led two great stands against the Japanese and his troops suffered terrible casualties. Then, however, he withdrew to Chungking in the heart of southern China and from 1939 the Kuomintang undertook no major campaigns against the Japanese.

In December 1941 the Japanese bombed the American naval base at Pearl Harbor in the Hawaiian Islands and the United States entered World War II. This meant that China once again had an important role to play in world politics. The Americans and the British flew supplies over the Himalayas to Chiang Kaishek's hideout in remote Chungking in order to help him against the Japanese. But Chiang had no intention of fighting the Japanese. All he wanted was to defeat the communists. His sister-in-law said in 1943: ''My brother-in-law is keeping the guns the Americans have given him in grease until they have beaten the Japanese for him. Then he will unwrap them for the war in which he is really interested, against the communists.''

Chiang was quite content to wait in the mountains while his enemies destroyed each other. He did not even help the Red Army with supplies and men. Indeed, in 1941 Chiang actually ordered the Kuomintang to resume their attacks on the Red Army.

Nevertheless, Mao soldiered on and his guerilla troops inflicted much damage on the Japanese. By 1945, when the Japanese retreated from China and surrendered, the Red Army, which, with its supporters, numbered over a million men, controlled several hundred square kilometres of Chinese territory. Mao could not claim, however, that the Red Army had freed China through its own efforts. The Japanese were forced to retreat mainly because of the American attacks on their empire and the two atom bombs dropped on Japan itself in 1945.

The Japanese invaders had been driven from China after nearly fifteen years; but foreign influence, which Mao had always detested, remained.

Below The Japanese attack on Pearl Harbor in 1941. This incident brought the United States into World War II.

10. Driving out the Kuomintang

Now the foreigners who influenced China were the Americans. Their aims were to help Chiang Kai-shek to power. Signs of this were clear as early as 1945. Although the communist troops were in an ideal position to drive out the Japanese forces in the north, the Americans flew in Kuomintang troops from Chungking to do the job instead. By the end of 1945 the Kuomintang controlled the major towns north of the Yangtze and all the area to its south. The communists were left holding the countryside north of the Yangtze.

At first, it is true, the Americans tried to keep the peace, and Mao was willing to co-operate. He told Robert Payne in 1946: "From the beginning up to now we have desired peace and we do not want this war prolonged." This was his plan: first he would join the Kuomintang in a coalition government. Then, the corruption and inefficiency of the Kuomintang would allow him to take over the leadership of China.

Chiang Kai-shek invited Mao to Chungking for discussions. On his way there Mao said: "Mr Chiang considers that, in general, there cannot be two suns in the sky nor can a people have two sovereigns. But I don't care; I am determined to give him two suns to look at."

But the meeting was unsuccessful, and Mao returned to Yenan in disgust. "He treated me like a peasant," he said later.

The two men were still firmly opposed. Chiang Kai-

"**Do the working people of China still look like slaves as they did in the past? No, they have become the masters. The working people ... have really begun to rule this land.**" *From* The Political Thought of Mao Tse-tung *by Stuart Schram.*

Opposite Mao rides into battle against Chiang Kai-shek during the civil war, 1947.

57

Right Mao at work in his cave study in Yenan in 1946. Sometimes he would read and write by candlelight, going without sleep or meals for days on end.

58

Above Mao reviewing the tank forces of the PLA near Peking in 1949, the year the communists came to power.

shek was determined to crush the Red Army and Mao was certainly not prepared to be crushed. Civil war was inevitable, and Mao made his feelings clear. He wrote: "All Chinese without exception must lean either to the side of imperialism or to the side of socialism. Sitting on the fence will not do, nor is there a third road." The Americans made their choice—they offered their support to Chiang Kai-shek.

Ironically, the Americans and their aid actually hastened Chiang's fall. The weapons intended for the Kuomintang were captured by the communists. In fact, if it had not been for the American arms, the communists would have had few reliable arms at all! They seized power not because of their own strength, but because of their opponent's weakness. Because of the incompetence of Chiang's government, Mao found himself kicking against an open door.

During his regime, Chiang had allowed China's economy to slide into ruin. Inflation rocketed. It required a suitcase full of bank-notes to pay for a restaurant meal. Money lost all meaning and trade was conducted by barter. Chiang's regime was also full of corruption. While thousands of Kuomintang troops were dying of gangrene and tuberculosis, Chiang's officials were making a huge profit selling American medical supplies on the black market.

Poverty became a fatal epidemic. When China suffered one of her regular famines, starvation reached a horrifying level. An American relief worker wrote of his own shocking experiences: "Millions of people are dying of starvation. They're eating earth and the barks of trees.... They're going crazy. They're killing children and eating them.... They're exchanging children for other people's so they don't have to kill their own."

Mao was not slow to accuse Chiang of letting thousands of children starve, while the businessmen who supported him grew fatter and fatter.

Chiang could only keep control of China by turning it into a police state. His methods of keeping control were ruthless and terrifying. They included the use of secret police, night-time executions, beatings-up in the streets and heavy censorship.

Meanwhile, Mao's regime was winning support in the same way that it had done in the soviets of Kiangsi and Shensi. Land was taken from the landlords and given

"We stand for self-reliance ... we depend on our own efforts, on the creative power of the whole army and the entire people." *From* The Thoughts of Chairman Mao.

Below China suffered from frequent famines. Here peasants are starving in the bare countryside.

to the peasants. Rents were reduced and farming methods improved. Attempts were made to develop industry. The Chinese under communist control could not fail to be impressed by the fairness and justice of Mao's rule, particularly compared to the tyranny of the Kuomintang. The party leaders and the peasants were treated as equals. Drives against illiteracy were launched. Laws against child slavery and compulsory marriage were passed. While the Politburo (the ruling committee) of the CCP made all the important laws, people's councils were set up to administer them and deal with local affairs.

To Mao, winning the hearts of the people was as essential as winning on the battlefield. One of his most famous sayings was: "The revolutionary war is a war of the masses; it can only be waged by mobilizing the masses and relying on them."

In 1948 the newly-named People's Liberation Army launched its attack. Chiang's resistance melted away as huge numbers of the Kuomintang army deserted. The attack became a rout. On an average day three towns surrendered, many of them without a shot being fired. Just before Shanghai fell to the victorious communists, Chiang took off in a plane loaded with booty for the island of Formosa (now called Taiwan). He remained there until his death in 1975, waiting hopelessly to "liberate" China.

On 1st October, 1949, the new communist government of the Peoples' Republic of China held a victory parade in Peking. The Chairman of the new Central Government Council, Mao Tse-tung, declared: "The Chinese people, one quarter of the human race, have now stood up." The country with the biggest population in the world had become a communist state.

11. Mao and the People's Will

The People's Republic of China has now existed for over a quarter of a century. During this time it has moved slowly and uneasily towards communism—that ideal state in which everyone works according to his ability and receives according to his needs; in which everyone freely gives up his possessions for the common good; and in which, because everybody is equal and in agreement, the people rule themselves and the state "withers away".

As in all other so-called "communist" states China is still in a state of socialism, a half-way stage between capitalism, where everyone works for his own good, and communism. The government rules on behalf of the people, organizing production (agriculture and industry), distribution (transport) and exchange (the banks) so that the country can become wealthy and its wealth can be distributed fairly among its people.

This change-over has not been easy, and Mao Tse-tung did not build Red China without brutality. Perhaps over one million landlords and "counter-revolutionaries" were executed between 1949–51. Mao made no apologies for this: "A revolution is not the same as inviting people to dinner ... to put it bluntly, it was necessary to bring about a brief reign of terror in every rural area; otherwise one could never suppress the activities of the counter-revolutionaries in the countryside or overthrow the authority of the gentry."

> **"The people, and the people alone, are the motive force in the making of world history."** *From* The Thoughts of Chairman Mao.

Opposite Group discussions in which everyone criticizes everyone else are common in China. Here women textile workers study and discuss communist posters.

Mao, however, was not a cruel man and his revolution brought far less physical suffering to China than Lenin's and Stalin's had to Russia. Mao was an optimist and a visionary. His vision was of a communist man selflessly devoted to society; his optimism led him to believe that he could make the Chinese become communists of their own free will. In other words he believed that, while Russian socialism was built by the passive obedience of the people, Chinese communism could be built through the co-operation of the masses. Where Lenin and Stalin used terror, Mao used persuasion.

He was a dictator all the same. Mao knew that Chinese-style persuasion amounted to an effective form of tyranny. The Chinese who did not share his ambitions had little chance to disagree, even though there were no secret police and no repressive code of laws such as there are under most dictatorships. The tyranny, in fact, took the form of popular pressure. The majority of Chinese imposed their will on the minority. Right from the start the majority shared Mao's determination to insist on discipline, even though they knew this meant giving up their freedom. They echoed Sun Yat-sen's statement: "We have become a tray of loose sand. We must break down individual liberty and become pressed together into an unyielding body like the firm rock which is formed by the addition of cement."

How does this persuasion work? How is discipline maintained? Partly by the use of propaganda. Propaganda is the publishing and broadcasting of information with strong emphasis on one point of view. It forms an ever-present background to people's lives. Day in and day out, in posters and on the radio, the people are urged to be brave, obedient, active, selfless and pure. Persuasion is also provided by members of the Chinese Communist Party and soldiers of the People's Liberation Army. They hold daily classes which consist of lectures, plays and recitations from the *Thoughts of Chairman Mao.*

As well as this, however, there is another form of persuasion—group discussions. These are sessions in which everyone can criticize everyone else, and himself too. The sessions take the form of people confessing in public to crimes against the spirit of communism. The group organizers play on the people's sense of loyalty to the Party, and on their feelings of hatred and shame. "Hatred", said Prime Minister Chou En-lai, "is a powerful social lever;" so is shame, for in China to "lose face" has always been a terrible insult.

"You can have no idea how agonizing these group meetings can be," a Chinese intellectual told Edgar Snow. "Everybody in my bureau from the office boy or scrubwoman up can tell me how bourgeois [middle or upper class] I am, criticize my personal habits, my family life, my intellectual arrogance, the way I spend my leisure, even my silences. I have to sit and take it. Some people prefer suicide rather than submit to it."

This constant "thought reform" or "brain-washing" is very effective. Edgar Snow noticed that a prison he visited was easy to escape from. "We've had several runaways in the past year," the prison superintendent told him. "Usually they are brought back by their families." Mao is reported to have told Stalin that the purges Stalin carried out during the thirties were wrong. "What you need are spiritual purges," he said.

There is, of course, a far more positive side to this persuasion and propaganda. Mao believed that the people's will is their source of strength. If the people's will-power can be harnessed it can then be released in an upsurge of revolutionary energy.

By looking at the rural communes, which are the central feature of Chinese communism, we can see just how the people's will-power has been harnessed to attempt truly mighty tasks.

> **"The young people are the most active and vital force in society. They are the most eager to learn and the least conservative in their thinking."** *From* The Thoughts of Chairman Mao.

12. Mao and the People's Communes

On 29th August, 1958, the Central Committee of the Chinese Communist Party made an earth-shaking announcement: "It seems that the attainment of communism in China is no longer a remote event. We should actively use the form of the people's communes to explore the practical road of transition to communism."

Mao's sudden decision to re-organize Chinese life into "people's communes", thereby bringing nearer his utopia of communism, became known as the "Great Leap Forward". After nearly ten years of socialism he had decided that the revolutionary drive of the Chinese people needed reviving. Men with the true revolutionary spirit, thought Mao, could work miracles. Now he was daring enough to put this to the test.

Up to this time there had been a gradual policy in China of giving "land to the tillers". First, land had been taken from the landlords and shared out among the peasants. Then this privately-owned land had been pooled into collective farms (farms in which the farmers share the land and its produce). Now these "collectives" were to be joined into larger units called "communes". China's 500 million peasants were to be grouped into 24,000 communes, each including about 100 villages and sometimes a local town. The idea of the commune was to combine economic efficiency with effective government. It was also expected to help organize its

> "What is a true bastion of iron? It is the masses, the millions upon millions of people who genuinely and sincerely support the revolution. That is the real bastion which it is impossible, and absolutely impossible, for any force on earth to smash." *From* The Thoughts of Chairman Mao.

Opposite The pin-up picture inspiring these tea pickers in Chekiang Province is Mao himself, in a peasant's hat.

own military power, security, finance, law and industry. In every-day matters the commune would be a self-governing unit.

The basic policy of the communes, however, was to: "complete the building of socialism ahead of time, and carry out the gradual transition to communism. . . . After a number of years . . . Chinese society will enter into the era of communism where the principle from each according to his ability and to each according to his needs will be practised."

In other words, wages and private property would eventually be replaced by the free supply of goods, and class distinctions would disappear.

The peasants of Hunan put this more poetically:

Below These stacks are made of cotton. Members of a commune in Hupeh Province are delivering and selling their crop to the state.

Setting up a people's commune is like going to
    heaven,
The achievements of a single night surpass those of
    several millenia
The sharp knife severs the roots of private property
Opening a new historical era.

The communes got under way, spurred on by Mao's
leadership. The Chinese masses, or "blue ants", as
foreigners nicknamed them because of their blue
overalls, forged ahead. Some of the new commune
leaders were so enthusiastic that they immediately
began to supply goods to the peasants free of charge.
On the other hand they also forced the peasants to give
up all their property for common use—even their pots
and pans. Thinking that the commune should replace
the family in the peasants' affections they built not only
communal nurseries and mess halls but separate dormi-
tories for all men and women too. By November 1958
many communes had been set up.

At the same time, and with the same enthusiasm, the
"blue ants" tried to fulfil the other objective of Mao's
Great Leap Forward. This was to use the large units
of labour in the new communes to develop China's industry by human effort instead of by mechanization.
Mao's target certainly required a superhuman leap. Its
aim in 1958 was to catch up with British industrial production in ten years and overtake America's in fifteen
or twenty years.

An example of the mammoth tasks undertaken by
peasants with their bare hands was given by this Shanghai commune director in 1964: "We have dug irrigation
canals which required 100,000 labour days. . . . We have
built 52 concrete bridges for our 16 large tractors and
built 6 miles of road. . . . We do our rice threshing by
machine and have built three 60-horse-power boats to
transport the rice."

Where they lacked machinery the peasants used their inventiveness. Edgar Snow saw motor-driven machines made entirely of wooden parts. He heard that workers had invented a stuffing machine for dressing cooked ducks, a noodle-making machine and a bill-counting machine!

It would indeed have been a miracle if Mao's Great Leap Forward had achieved its two aims of communism and economic prosperity. The real result, in a phrase once used by Lenin, was that the Chinese took "two steps forward and one step back". Economically, China is still far behind the west but the communists have eliminated starvation and dire poverty—a huge achievement if we remember that Mao's government took over a poor country made poorer by quarter of a century of war and destruction. By 1960 the intense activity of the Great Leap Forward had died down. The energies of the Chinese people are now harnessed into a steadier programme of development.

As for the achievement of communism, Mao's idealistic communes have not, so far, changed human nature. The Chinese peasant has not been prepared to become a selfless communist man to the extent of giving up all his land and his household. The commune directors have now recognized this and returned to the peasant his own house (rented free) and private garden. Most important, the peasant is paid according to how much he works rather than according to how much he needs. However, each commune promises its peasants "five guarantees"—care for those too old to work, adequate food, shelter and clothing, fuel, medical care and a proper burial. This must seem like a miracle to those old enough to remember their lives before 1949.

Mao said that he expected the fight for communism to go on "for a hundred, a thousand, nay, ten thousand years". Who knows whether his "revolutionary romanticism" will eventually triumph?

Opposite Young people are often sent out into the countryside. Here a girl from Shanghai helps a commune member to study Mao's works.

13. Mao and the Red Guards

Betweeen 1966 and 1968 Mao Tse-tung launched the third major stage of his revolution to turn China into the world's first communist state. The first stage, achieved in 1949, was political—the Kuomintang was overthrown and the Chinese Communist Party, the champion of the masses, came to power. The second stage, most marked between 1958 and 1961, was economic—the capitalist economy was replaced by a socialist one and the communes were set up.

The third stage was to be cultural. Mao intended to alter the whole philosophy of the Chinese people so that they became communists in mind as well as in body. This "Cultural Revolution", as it was called, involved a build-up of the "thought reform" that the Chinese had been subjected to for the previous twenty years. At times the propaganda and persuasion were so intense that people became hysterical and the revolution got out of control.

Mao's troops for fighting the Cultural Revolution were the Red Guards. These were enthusiastic teenagers specially trained for the task under Mao's direction.

Their training began at school, where they were given a "socialist education". This education, which is still normal in Chinese schools today, aims to convert children towards complete faith in Chinese communism.

In 1976 an English newspaper reporter was being

> **"Without a people's army the people have nothing."** *From* The Thoughts of Chairman Mao.

Opposite Mao doffs his cap and Red Guards wave their "Little Red Books" in Peking, 1975.

shown round the Hsin Hua primary school in Peking. Round the class-room walls were prize essays on the theme "Never forget the Revolution." There were pictures of Mao Tse-tung in every classroom and text books were all altered to show the latest government thinking.

The reporter discovered that all pupils spent three weeks every five months working on farms or in factories to learn respect for the "dignity of labour". The headmaster, known as the Chairman of the Revolutionary Council, told him that "the main aim of the children's education is political." The reporter asked what would happen if a pupil did not want to become a Red Guard. The headmaster replied that first the teacher would try and "correct" his attitude; if this failed he would be subjected to "mass criticism" by his classmates; then he would be sent to the bottom of the class.

Chinese children have been given public duties since the early days of the revolution, as this example from the *Peking Review* of 1958 shows: "A man, while strolling along the street, suddenly spat. He was immediately approached by a little girl who politely asked him if he had spat. The man admitted that he had.... The girl was a member of a Health Inspection Team which was doing its part in the campaign against spitting."

The Cultural Revolution gave the Red Guards the opportunity to demonstrate the effectiveness of their "socialist education". Mao now placed his hope in them as he used them to attempt the third stage of his revolution.

His targets were the "revisionaries". These were the people who were accused of wanting to go back to the early days of the revolution. They were peasants who were too attached to their own property, intellectuals who were too fond of Western ideas, or members of the CCP who gave themselves privileges and wanted power for its own sake. All these revisionaries were Mao's enemies.

Mao also had personal reasons for starting the Cultural Revolution. Since the partial failure of his Great Leap Forward he had lost some of his power. In 1959 he resigned from the Chairmanship of the People's Republic, although he retained his Chairmanship of the CCP. The Cultural Revolution was his way of fighting back. He knew that this third revolution might destroy the very organization on which Chinese communism had been built—the CCP itself. To Mao in the long run, this did not matter. "In the last analysis", he said, "all the truths of communism can be summed up in one sentence: To rebel is justified."

Mao first assembled his Red Guards in Peking in August 1966. It was estimated that about eleven million Red Guards travelled to Peking to be encouraged by Mao. Then, carrying the "Little Red Book" which contained the thoughts of Chairman Mao and encouraged by Mao's motto "dare to do", they went out into China to weed out revisionaries and preach communism.

For the next eighteen months they campaigned violently against his revisionary targets. They threw furniture out of private houses, ordered shopkeepers not to sell Western fashions and destroyed the private gardens of rich peasants. They humiliated thousands of party officials by forcing them to wear dunces' caps and carry rude placards around their necks. They caused about half the number of ministers and high officials to resign. "Mao has done a better job in destroying his own party than Chiang Kai-shek," said one American observer.

The chaos of the Cultural Revolution might have caused the collapse of the system that Mao had set up. In the end Mao had to call out the People's Liberation Army and launch another campaign of propaganda to calm the Red Guards down.

Opposite A 100-kilometre long aqueduct built to irrigate farmland in Hopei Province.

Below New Students going to Tsinghua University to learn science and engineering. They are workers, peasants and soldiers with practical experience, and will go back to their old jobs later.

How successful was the Cultural Revolution? There is no doubt that the eagerness of the Red Guards got out of hand. Nevertheless the Revolution reminded the Chinese people most forcibly of their communist goal. It was also a tactical victory for Mao. By turning the Red Guards and the PLA against the CCP he had disobeyed one of his own rules—"the Party commands the gun, the gun must never be allowed to command the Party." However, the result was that his enemies in the Party were expelled and future events were to show that the army could still be controlled by the Party.

Mao's own verdict was: "We cannot speak lightly of final victory, not even for decades." Further revolutions, he said, will be necessary to renew the enthusiasm of the young and prevent the laziness of the old. For Mao, the incurable rebel, "disequilibrium [disorder] is normal and absolute, whereas equilibrium [order] is temporary and relative."

Mao greeting Dr Henry
Kissinger, US Secretary of State,
in 1975.

14. Mao the Statesman

Mao continued to greet visiting statesmen until 1976. It was on these occasions that cameramen showed to the world that Chairman Mao, though visibly ageing, was still capable of discussing—perhaps making—foreign policy with his guests.

These meetings sometimes took place in Mao's modest one-storey house in Peking. The camera would show Mao's study, with its shelves laden with books and the desk piled high with papers. Through the wide windows the camera would pick out Mao's garden, where the Chairman was said to grow his own vegetables and experiment with crops. Mao ceased to administer China's foreign policy some years before his death. Nevertheless, his influence over it remains today.

For half a century Mao's attitude to the world outside China was shaped by his attitude towards Russia. It was an attitude which passed from admiration through mistrust to hostility. His first visit to Russia in 1949, which was his first visit outside China, was not a good starting-point for future relations. Stalin and the other Russian leaders kept him at a distance and treated him rather as if he was a dangerous pet.

When Stalin died in 1953, Mao probably expected to succeed him as the acknowledged head of world communism. When Nikita Khrushchev—Stalin's successor—did not pay him this respect Mao did not forgive the Russians. Of course there are other, more basic

> **"Riding roughshod everywhere, US imperialism has made itself the enemy of the people of the world and has increasingly isolated itself."** *From* The Thoughts of Chairman Mao.

Above Chiang Ch'ing, Mao's fourth wife. An actress once known as "Blue Apple", she married Mao at Yenan. After Mao's death she was imprisoned for trying to seize power.

reasons for the hostility between the two countries. They have a long history of border disputes and of arguments over which country is more truly communist. Yet it is significant that Mao always regarded himself as a great teacher, and the Russian leaders never treated him as if he was.

The United States of America was the other country towards which much of Mao's foreign policy was directed. Until quite recently the two countries were open enemies. It is easy to see why. America had supported the Kuomintang and after 1949 continued to back Chiang Kai-shek, now marooned on Taiwan. A powerful group of American businessmen and politicians, who stood to gain from Chiang's return to power, made the most of America's fear of communism and anger at Mao's success. Indeed, the American Navy patrolled the sea around Taiwan, preventing Mao from achieving what he wanted most. This was to conquer his old enemy and complete his revolution. Chinese and American troops actually clashed during the Korean war, and when it was reported that the United Nations commander General MacArthur wanted to bomb China many people expected a total war between the two countries. It was certainly no secret that the USA hoped for the collapse of Mao's regime and the restoration of Chiang's.

Perhaps the single event which did most to bring the two countries to the conference table was China's explosion of an atom bomb in 1964. Now America had to recognize China as a world power. This recognition came, slowly but surely. In 1971 Mao's China was admitted to the United Nations and Chiang's China was expelled. America also withdrew her fleet from the Straits of Taiwan. Then in 1972 the United States President, Richard Nixon, visited Mao. The two leaders discussed what in diplomatic language means an armed truce—"peaceful co-existence". Taiwan, however, remained as a rebel island. Mao must have been insulted when Chiang insisted on calling the island "The Republic of China".

This did not mean that Mao's real attitude to the USA changed. He always regarded America as a modern Kuomintang on an international scale—an imperialist power which must be resisted by guerilla war. But just as he had set aside his differences with the Kuomintang in order to fight the Japanese, so he was prepared to set aside his differences with America in order to concentrate on what he considered to be a more immediate threat—Russia.

It must be remembered, however, that nothing in Mao's teaching or thought ever called for a war against America or for any other war of foreign conquest; nor did Mao ever place faith in atom bombs. As we saw early in his life's story, Mao was a nationalist at heart, but a nationalist whose aim was to protect China rather than to build a Chinese empire.

We have also seen that Mao was a military and political revolutionary. This influenced the third area of his foreign policy, the area outside the big power blocks known as the Third World. Some years ago the then Chinese Minister of Defence, Lin Piao, made a famous speech calling on the "exploited" countries of Asia, Africa and Latin America to make "revolutions against America". What he meant was that those countries which were dominated by American power—economic, military or political power—should win their independence by waging guerilla war, just as the Chinese communists had done against the Kuomintang. Mao believed in this strongly. He said that China would support revolutionary struggle "in the interests of China and the whole world". He also said, however, that each country must be liberated as a result of its own efforts.

When Mao died on 9th September, 1976, the reactions from other countries reflected his foreign

Above China has been an important influence on Albania. Here young Albanians are reading about the cultural revolution.

policies. President Ford of the USA paid tribute: "Chairman Mao was a giant figure in modern Chinese history," he announced. The Russians, on the other hand, paid no tribute. The Taiwanese were delighted. One newspaper cartoon showed Mao on his way to hell, another a fly-covered corpse. Messages of sympathy from the Third World poured into Peking.

No cause was given for Mao's death. As he was eighty-two perhaps none was needed. It is worth noting that the four men who, arguably, did most to make Chinese history over the last half-century died within the space of a few months. Chiang Kai-shek was the first to die, in 1975, followed early in 1976 by Chou En-lai and then Chu Teh. The greatest of the four died last. His death brought to an end the most extraordinary era in China's long history.

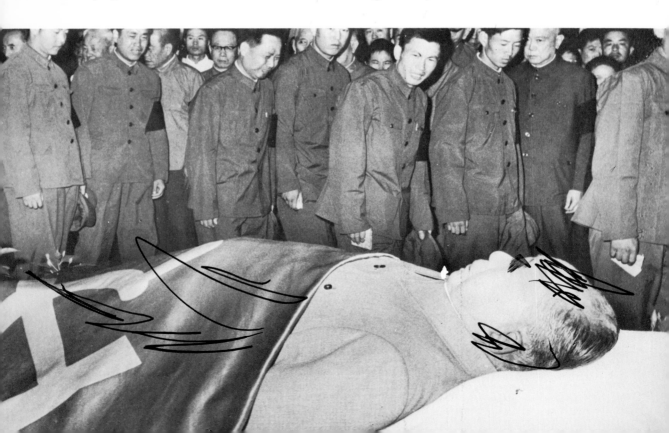

Below Mao lying in state in Peking, 1976. Soldiers of the People's Liberation Army file past wearing mourning bands and weeping.

15. The Myth of Mao

A few years ago an Australian writer travelling through China wrote this: "In the environs [suburbs] of Nanking, I saw roadside altars turned into little shrines of Mao Tse-tung Thought; the central tablet was redone in red, featuring the star of the CCP, and quotations from the Chairman ran in strips from top to bottom down each side."

In the same way, he was startled to meet people like this: "I met a railway worker who'd been hit by a train and the resulting spine disorder paralysed him from the waist down so that he had lain in bed like a vegetable for eighteen years. In the Cultural Revolution when doctors were urged to tackle 'even the impossible', a team at the hospital began acupuncture treatment.... [Now] the worker hobbled across the room on crutches to greet me and said: 'I am out of bed because of Chairman Mao's Thought. Soon I will go back to work for the sake of the revolution.'"

Mao Tse-tung, the Australian realized, had become a myth in his own lifetime. People prayed to him as to a living God. He was expected to work miracles. In this sense it matters little whether Mao is alive or dead. Indeed, the Chinese now plan to preserve his body for ever. It is to be kept in a crystal coffin a few hundred yards from the spot where he founded the Chinese People's Republic in 1949.

During his lifetime Mao took on a super-human

> **"The people who have triumphed in their own revolution should help those still struggling for liberation. This is our internationalist duty."** *From* The Thoughts of Chairman Mao.

> **"A dangerous tendency has shown itself of late among many of our personnel—an unwillingness to share the joys and hardships of the masses, a concern for personal fame and gain. This is very bad."** *From* The Thoughts of Chairman Mao.

status which has continued to inspire the Chinese after his death. A. L. Rowse, one of our greatest historians, wrote of him in 1975 as "by far the greatest man in the world today—probably the greatest of this century". How did Mao become such a myth?

We must remember that for the three thousand years before this century, the Chinese worshipped their emperor. As a result it was hard for the simple peasants to break this habit when Mao came to power. A Chinese intellectual told Edgar Snow: "During the early years of the revolution . . . when the peasants came to Peking to celebrate the anniversary and went past the reviewing stand, many bowed low before Chairman Mao. We had to keep guards there to stop them from prostrating themselves."

Soon afterwards, when Edgar Snow met Mao, he asked him what he thought of this "personality cult". Mao acknowledged that it existed and said that perhaps there were good reasons for it. "Probably Mr Khrushchev fell [from power] because he had no cult of personality at all," he said. Mao did not discourage this worship. He knew that it would make it harder for his enemies to get rid of him.

Mao's achievements were so extraordinary that simple people could be forgiven for thinking that he was indeed a super-human capable of working miracles. In the seventy years of Mao's adult life he saw changes which in other parts of the world took two centuries to come about. He was more responsible for these changes than anybody else. At the beginning of this century China was a backward and despised empire; its army was weak, its economy poor, its people terribly oppressed. Now, as a result of his life's work, China is a new nation. It is one of the world's great powers, and is respected and feared by other nations. Its armed forces and its economy are strong and its people are more healthy, educated, happy and equal than ever

Above The Memorial Hall for Mao under construction. It will contain Mao's preserved remains in a crystal coffin.

seemed possible. No wonder the peasants build their little red shrines to Mao Tse-tung Thought.

We should also remember that it is Mao's Thought that is worshipped as much as Mao himself. For Mao was a great teacher, with a special skill for teaching simple people. One of his methods was to use folk myths to get across his political message. For example, in 1945 he wrote a story called *The Foolish Old Man Who Removed the Mountains*. Based on a Chinese myth, it tells the story of a farmer who attempted the impossible. He tried to dig away, with his two sons, two mountains that crowded in on his house. Ridiculed by wise men, he persisted, saying that more generations and more sons would carry on the work they were beginning, and eventually they would succeed. And so, in the myth, they did—with the help of the gods. In his story Mao likened the two mountains to the two evils blocking China's progress—feudalism and imperialism; the gods became "the masses" who, digging together, would clear the way. And so, thirty years after the Civil War, they have done.

As Mao used these old myths to inspire the peasants and convert them to communism, it is easy to see how some of the events in his own life, events such as the Long March, have become myths themselves which serve the same purpose. Mao is proud of his title "Great Teacher". He said to Edgar Snow in 1965 that he had started life as a teacher and was one still. His other titles of "Great Leader", "Great Helmsman" and "Great Supreme Commander" were a nuisance, he said, but he hoped his title of "Great Teacher" would continue. It is reasonable to say that *The Thoughts of Chairman Mao*, published in The Little Red Book, are to the Chinese what the sayings of Jesus Christ in the Bible are to Christians—and they are as powerful now as they were two thousand years ago.

Mao himself did not think his influence would last that long. He once said: "The world is changing very rapidly and we cannot decide what its future generations will do. A thousand years from now all of us, even Marx and Lenin, will probably appear ridiculous."

Mao was a simple man but his thinking was often difficult to understand. Now he is dead one of his most puzzling policies will be put to the test. As Chairman of the CCP since 1935 and father of the Republic since 1949, Chairman Mao was the greatest unifying force in China. Yet, as we have noticed throughout his life story, he was also a "romantic revolutionary" whose motto was "to rebel is justified". Mao, in fact, often encouraged rebellion. Will the myth of Mao now hold China together or will the disruptive influence of his life tear China apart? Perhaps both will happen, and the puzzle will be solved. As Mao himself might have put it, perhaps China will move from a stable position to an unstable position, from which a new stability will emerge.

Opposite The people of China worshipped Mao in his lifetime, and openly showed their grief when he died. This is a mass memorial rally of three hundred thousand mourners in Lanchow, Kansu Province.

Principal Characters

Chiang Ch'ing (1913?   ). Mao's fourth wife (third if his childhood bride is not counted); formerly a film star known as Lan-ping ("Blue Apple"); later Mao's tough and trusted lieutenant, particularly during the Cultural Revolution. After Mao's death she was imprisoned for trying to seize power. She claimed that she was following Mao's instructions to continue the revolution.

Chiang Kai-shek (1887–1975). Mao's life-long rival; formerly Generalissimo of the Republic of China and leader of the Kuomintang; later President of Nationalist China on Taiwan.

Chou En-lai (1898–1976). Appointed General Political Director of the Red Army during the Long March; Communist China's first Prime Minister and Foreign Minister and Mao's indispensable ally. He kept the government going during the Cultural Revolution.

Chu Teh (1886–1976). Founded the Kiangsi soviet with Mao; Commander in Chief of the First Front Army during the Long March; Vice-Chairman of Communist China 1950–9.

Lin Piao (1908–71). Commanded the 1st Army Corps on the Long March; Defense Minister of Communist China and Mao's chosen successor; led the People's Liberation Army behind Mao in the Cultural Revolution; accused of plotting to assassinate Mao and killed, allegedly, in a plane crash in Mongolia.

Mao Tse-tung (1893–1976). Guerilla expert, philosopher, poet and prophet, peasant leader; founding father of Communist China and Chairman of the Chinese Communist Party 1935–76.

Sun Yat-sen (1866–1925). Founder of the Kuomintang and President of the First Chinese Republic.

Table of Dates

1893 26th December: Mao Tse-tung born in Shao Shan, Hunan province.

1911 Mao becomes a student at Changsha middle school.

   October: Outbreak of revolution leading to overthrow of Manchu dynasty.

1918 Autumn: Mao becomes a library assistant in Peking.

1920 Mao organizes a communist group in Hunan.

1921 July: Mao attends the First Congress of the Chinese Communist Party in Shanghai.

   October: Mao becomes Secretary of the CCP for Hunan.

1925 Death of Sun Yat-sen and start of Chiang Kai-shek's leadership of the Kuomintang.

1927 April: The Kuomintang attack their communist allies in Shanghai and start the Civil War.

1928 Chiang Kai-shek captures Peking and becomes Generalissimo of China.

1929 Mao and Chu Teh establish their soviet in Kiangsi.

1930 November: Chiang Kai-shek launches his First Annihilation Campaign.

1931 September: Japanese attack Manchuria.

1934 October: Start of the Long March to escape the Fifth Annihilation Campaign.

1935	January:	Mao made Chairman of the CCP.
	October:	Red Army links up with communists in Shensi, ending its Long March.
1936	August:	Mao suggests alliance with Kuomintang against Japanese, followed by "Sian Incident" in which Chiang is captured and delivered to Mao.
1937		Chiang accepts offer and agrees to the Three Great Objectives.
1939		Kuomintang retreats from war against Japanese.
1941	December:	Japanese attack Pearl Harbor and Americans send aid to Chinese.
1945		Japanese withdraw from China; Mao attempts, unsuccessfully, to negotiate with Chiang.
1948		Mao announces an offensive on all fronts against the Kuomintang.
1949	October:	Mao proclaims establishment of the Chinese People's Republic.
	November:	Chiang Kai-shek establishes Nationalist China in Taiwan.
	December:	Mao visits Moscow and meets Stalin.
1950		Intervention of Chinese in Korea.
1951		Mao begins land reform and launches "thought reform" campaigns.
1953		End of Korean War.
1958		Launching of the Great Leap

	Forward; Mao advocates the creation of communes and the mobilization of the masses to produce steel.
1959	Retreat from the Great Leap Forward; Mao ceases to be Chairman of the Republic of China.
1966 August:	Mao reviews the Red Guards in Peking and launches the Cultural Revolution.
1968	After intervention by the PLA, the Cultural Revolution is ended.
1969	Serious clashes between Chinese and Russian troops on their common border.
1971	Communist China admitted to United Nations; Nationalist China expelled.
1972	President of USA, Richard Nixon, visits China and meets Mao.
1976 September:	Death of Mao Tse-tung.

Further Reading

All these books are intended for the general reader. Most of them are suitable for readers in the intended age range of this book (14–16-year-olds).

A Short History of China by Hilda Hookham (Longman, 1969). A good introduction.

Red Star Over China by Edgar Snow (Pelican, 1972). This is essential reading. First published in 1937 it includes Mao's virtual autobiography as told to the author in Yenan. It is highly readable.

Red China Today by Edgar Snow (Pelican, 1970). This is the sequel to *Red Star Over China*, equally readable and almost as important. No westerner knew Mao as well as the author.

China's Long Revolution by Edgar Snow (Pelican, 1974). This was the author's last book written after his last visit to China and published after his death.

Mao Tse-tung by Stuart Schram (Pelican, 1966). This highly-respected biography is suitable for older readers.

Mao Tse-tung and China by C. P. FitzGerald (Hamish Hamilton, 1976). A short, up-to-date biography by a distinguished historian who has lived in China for several years.

The Long March 1935 by Dick Wilson (Hamish Hamilton, 1971). This is an extremely readable and full story of "The Epic of Chinese Communism's Survival". Particularly recommended to this age group.

A Quarter of Mankind: An Anatomy of China Today by Dick Wilson (Penguin, 1968).

The Thoughts of Chairman Mao Tse-tung (Anthony Gibbs, 1967). This is the western equivalent of the Little Red Book.

The Political Thought of Mao Tse-tung by Stuart Schram (Penguin, 1965). This is an edited collection of Mao's writings.

Mao Tse-tung and the Chinese Communist Revolution by Elizabeth Mauchline Roberts (Methuen Outlines, 1970). This is particularly recommended for the younger age group.

Index

Picture Credits

The author and publishers wish to thank all those who have given permission for the reproduction of copyright illustrations on the following pages: Radio Times Hulton Picture Library, 22, 26, 32, 45, 48, 52, 61; The Mansell Collection, 13, 14, 18–19, 21, 27, 29, 36, 55; Keystone Press Agency, 10, 63; Hsinhua News Agency, 15, 42; Anglo-Chinese Educational Institute, *frontispiece*, 8, 11, 24, 30, 33, 38–39, 46, 51, 54, 56, 58–59, 60, 64, 68, 70, 73, 74, 78, 79, 80, 82, 83, 84, 87, 89; the remaining pictures are the copyright of the Wayland Picture Library.